Anna, Jesus Loves You

Anna, Jesus Loves You

A Story of Healing and Hope

James K. Wagner

The Upper Room
Nashville, Tennessee

Anna, Jesus Loves You

Copyright © 1985 by The Upper Room.

Scripture quotations not otherwise identified are from the Revised Standard Version
of the Bible, copyrighted 1946, 1952 and © 1971 by the Division of Christian
Education, National Council of the Churches of Christ in the United States of
America, and are used by permission.

Scripture quotations designated NEB are from The New English Bible, © The
Delegates of the Oxford University Press and the Syndics of the Cambridge University Press 1961 and 1970, and are used by permission.

Excerpt from "Aspects of Recovery" in *A New Heart* (Vol. 7, No. 1) used by
permission of the author, Dr. William S. Jasper.

Excerpt from *The Upper Room Disciplines 1982*, copyright © 1981 by The Upper
Room. Used by permission.

Excerpts from *The Upper Room* (March/April 1982), copyright © 1981 by The Upper
Room, 1908 Grand Avenue, Nashville, Tennessee 37202. Used by permission.

Cover Design: Harriette Bateman
Book Design: Thelma Whitworth
First Printing: June, 1985 (5)
Library of Congress Catalog Number: 84–052231
ISBN: 0-8358-0512-3

Printed in the United States of America

Contents

To Anna's great-great-grandmother
Anna Blanche Wheatley Stone
Born 1889

*Her persevering Christian faith
is a strength and an inspiration
to all in her family.*

Foreword

"It is absurd to apologize for mystery." With this word Asher Lev puts into perspective the story of his life in *My Name is Asher Lev* by Chaim Potok. And what a truth!

The mystery of healing is baffling, but it is absurd to apologize for it. James Wagner knows that. In this beautiful story, he affirms and celebrates not only the healing of his granddaughter Anna, but the healing ministry of Christ and his church. He puts that celebration and affirmation where it belongs—in the context of the fact that "God has many delivery systems through which to channel health . . . wholeness" and salvation.

This is an inspiring story of love, family, extended family, church, prayer, healing—all centered around a little baby who was born with a serious heart problem. It is the story of the miracles of modern medical science and the story of faith and the spiritual power released through prayer.

In his previous book, *Blessed to Be a Blessing,* my friend Jim made a marvelous contribution to the healing ministry of the church. Now, in *Anna, Jesus Loves You,* he provides another helpful resource in this too-neglected area of our Christian life and the corporate life of the church. The book is more than a moving, well-written story that will inspire and bless you; it is solid, helpful, wholesome teaching on healing.

I'm happy that Jim has written Anna's story. I commend it heartily, and I'm delighted that it is being published as Jim completes his first year as the Director of the Prayer and Healing Ministries for The Upper Room.

Maxie D. Dunnam

Preface

A few years ago as I was sitting in an adult Sunday school class discussing many different kinds of tragedies that befall human beings, one of the men present began to share several tragic situations that his family had had to face, one on top of another. In his prayer life he found himself asking, "Why me, Lord? Why me?" To this, one of the women responded, "Why not me?"

Somewhere, somehow, many of us pick up the notion that if we live the right kind of life, believe the right kind of beliefs, do the right kind of deeds, then we will be exempt from the heartaches and sorrows that we see in the lives of some people who do not "follow the rules." This theology holds that God rewards the good with good lives and punishes the bad with bad lives. Even though that kind of religious thinking can be supported by certain passages in the Bible, life does not work out that neatly. Bad things do happen to good people every day.

Such is the case in our family. We are Bible-believing, church-going, tax-paying, law-abiding citizens trying to live out our Christianity. Yet we have discovered that this is no guarantee of a problem-free life and offers no exemptions to human suffering. In 1958, my wife's father, Dr. Lorin Stine, a minister in the Evangelical United Brethren Church and the pastor of a large, growing congregation in Dayton, Ohio, was killed along with two other ministers in a head-on automobile collision. The other car had crossed the double yellow line on a two-lane highway.

In our painful grief and personal loss, our family never once believed that this tragic circumstance was the will of God. Rather, we found ourselves in the fellowship of wounded human beings confronted with the fragility and insecurity of life.

This book is the story of our first grandchild, Anna Lucille Bujdoso. What happened to Anna the doctors cannot explain; probably no one can explain it. We did not find the answer to the "Why?" question simply by looking in the Bible. However, in dealing with Anna's situation, our family did find in the holy scripture some possible answers. We also learned how to cope and to whom we could turn in times of difficulty.

I have long believed the spiritual truth found in Romans 8:28: "We know that in everything God works for good with those who love him, who are called according to his purpose." I am convinced that God does not intentionally cause suffering, sickness, and tragedy. My experience informs me that in all and through all situations, God can and does produce good for those who love God and who turn to God in their weakness, frustration, disappointment, and discouragement. For Christians, this calls for a continual affirmation that we are not God; rather, God is God. God is our refuge, our fortress, our rock, our guiding force, our loving presence, our caring shepherd, our source of healing.

The God of abundant life and wholeness has provided us with many spiritual therapies to help and enhance our healing of body, mind, spirit, and relationships. In the church in which I was pastor, we had weekly services of holy communion with intentional prayers for healings. This, we discovered, is a very practical, helpful ministry in the total life of the congregation. With the birth of Anna and her unfortunate physical condition, our family and countless other Christians had an opportunity to use these spiritual therapies, not only for the baby's sake, but for all who were touched by this child of God.

Those first days after Anna's birth caused our family to rethink our theology, to renew our biblical faith, and to put into practice the spiritual concepts regarding Christianity that we had been taught and held as truth. The purpose of this book is not only to tell Anna's story, but also to share spiritual guidance with other families who are forced to cope with tragic and near-tragic circumstances in their lives.

One of the tenets of the Christian healing ministry is that God has many delivery systems through which to channel health and wholeness. One of those delivery systems is the medical profession. Our family is much indebted to the dozens of doctors, nurses, and other hospital personnel through whom God worked in helping Anna.

A special note of appreciation to Penrose Hospital in Colorado Springs, Colorado, to the nursing staff, and to pediatrician Dr. John H. Genrich. We also acknowledge with gratitude the University of Colorado Medical Center in Denver and, in particular, the neonatal care unit. There we witnessed and experienced the ministry of love and healing carried on twenty-four hours each day. We believe it was only through the specialized training and expertise of the pediatric cardiology team (Dr. James W. Wiggins, Dr. Robert R. Wolfe, and Dr. Larry T. Mahoney) that Anna's life was saved within the first week of her birth. We are also indebted to Dr. David R. Clarke, the pediatric heart surgeon. For helping me learn the correct medical terminology, I thank my good friend, Dr. John T. Huston, Director of Cardiology Services at Riverside Methodist Hospital in Columbus, Ohio.

With thankfulness our hearts also go out to the Reverend Dr. Lloyd Nichols, a resident of Colorado Springs and lifelong personal friend of our family, who just happened to be staying with his critically ill wife in the same hospital in which Anna was born. The Lord certainly worked through Lloyd as he ministered to our family in those crisis moments.

I do not know how people manage to cope with life without the everyday personal caring of Christian friends. Ours were with us in so many, many ways throughout this uncertain time, especially David and Joyce Warner of Columbus, Ohio. Their presence and prayers helped us more than they know.

For assisting in preparing the manuscript for this book, I thank my daughter Kerrie Wagner Zeuch and her friend Kim Bateman, who transcribed cassette tape recordings to the typewritten page; Betsy Paxton for retyping the completed manuscript; Sharon Perry for photocopying, mailing, and other necessary tasks; the Reverend David Maze family for giving an "objective" reading and evaluation of the book; Mrs. Freda Cassel, Anna's maternal great-grandmother, whose generosity lightened the heavy financial burden more than once; and to my wife and best friend Mary Lou, who now shares with me the joys of grandparenthood.

James K. Wagner

The Spirit helps us in our weakness; for we do not know how to pray as we ought, but the Spirit himself intercedes for us with sighs too deep for words.

—Romans 8:26

1
Ecstasy and Agony

"And, dear God, please help Laurie at the Dairy Queen. Amen." With this concern for his sister, our seven-year-old son Toby concluded his prayer at our evening meal. Our friend, David Cottrill, happened to be eating with us and was rather surprised by this prayer request.

"Toby, why did you pray for Laurie?" he asked.

"Well, you see, Laurie has a hard time at work. Sometimes she cries when she comes home. We can't be with her to help her—but God can," he answered rather matter-of-factly.

That was in the early 1970s when our family was just beginning the process of learning to pray and to trust God in all of our needs, fears, hurts, failures, inadequacies, illnesses, and anxieties. We took, and continue to take, seriously what I once heard Elton Trueblood say: "Whatever is worth worrying about is worth praying about." And so we prayed for teenage Laurie at the Dairy

Queen, for her younger sister, Kerrie, who was having a rough time in French class, for Toby and his neighborhood playmates, for my wife Mary Lou, a public school elementary music teacher, and for myself, a United Methodist pastor. We discovered that life does go more smoothly with prayer and that the Lord truly cares about our every need every day.

Laurie survived the Dairy Queen, graduated from Westland High School in a southwestern suburb of Columbus, Ohio, and went on to college. She attended Ohio Northern University in Ada, Ohio, where she earned a degree in social work and married Laszlo G. Bujdoso. Extremely sensitive to the needs of others, Laurie went to work on the medical social work staff at Memorial Hospital in Lima, Ohio. Daily she dealt with victims of rape and abuse, estranged families, poverty-stricken people, elderly patients with no families, and all sorts of other human problems.

In 1981 Laurie and Laszlo moved to Colorado Springs, Colorado, where he found employment in business and marketing. Soon the news came back to Ohio. Our first grandchild was due in the spring. Naturally we prayed for a healthy baby and a safe, uncomplicated delivery, knowing that God's love has no geographical limits. Because I was not present at the birth, I want Laurie to tell that part of our story.

Laurie Remembers Anna's Birth

The baby was born on March 28, 1982, at 3:30 A.M. in Penrose Hospital, Colorado Springs, Colorado. A much wanted birth. A full-term baby girl. She is the first grandchild on both sides of her family. I did everything I could think of to get ready. I never missed a doctor's appointment. I had ultrasound tests to be sure the fetus was developing normally. I took prenatal exercise classes and watched my diet carefully. I do not smoke or drink alcoholic beverages. My husband and I attended natural childbirth classes (Lamaze) for eight weeks. We wanted to be completely ready for the arrival of this child.

However, nothing in my reading or in my prenatal classes prepared me for what to do if the baby was not healthy and everything was not okay. Throughout my pregnancy, my doctor gave me good reports. The fetal heartbeat was strong, and the other monitoring tests were all positive. Never once did we suspect there could be a problem.

Because I was healthy and had such a confident attitude, my doctor and I decided ahead of time to use a birthing-chair for the delivery, rather than a bed. The birthing-chair was new to the Colorado Springs area. When I started having labor pains and checked into the hospital, I learned that not only was the birthing-chair new to that maternity ward, but that I would be the very first mother to use it. When the baby was born we had more people than usual in the delivery room. Several nurses and resident doctors wanted to see how the birthing-chair worked.

It worked fine. The moment the baby was born, she let the world know that she had arrived. Before she was completely delivered, as her head emerged, she yelled. I remember crying because I thought she was so beautiful—probably the most beautiful baby ever born, but I know that this is only a prejudiced mother's point of view. Laz and I had discussed names for six months before the birth, mostly boy names. In fact, we had decided what to call a boy baby but could not get together on a girl's name.

Immediately after the birth, I got to hold the baby for a few precious minutes. Then one of the nurses took her across the room to wash her and weigh her. Laz hugged me and said, "Congratulations! Now what are we going to name the baby?" Well, she certainly did not look like a James Ryan. I know Laz was surprised when I said to him, "The baby's name is Anna Lucille." She just looked like an Anna. I named her Anna after my great-grandmother Anna Blanche Wheatley Stone and Lucille after my mother Mary Lucille Stine Wagner.

Then they gave Anna to me and wheeled us to the recovery room. I remember the nurses telling me how healthy she was and what a pretty baby she was and that seven pounds, eleven ounces was not too big or too small. The recovery room was equipped with a telephone. Within minutes Laszlo, the proud father, was on the phone calling his parents in Lisbon, Ohio, and calling my relatives. I'll never forget talking to my father in Athens, Ohio, that morning. It was around 6:00 A.M. (his time) on a Sunday.

"Daddy, Daddy, she's beautiful! Her name is Anna Lucille. She's okay and so am I. Oh, Daddy, I'm so thankful. Now you can go to church and tell all the people."

"Laurie, this is great! You're beautiful. I love you."

"I love you, Daddy. Here's Mother."

"Hi! Guess what? I'm holding your granddaughter. She's beautiful. Everything is fine."

"That's great! Just great! I can't wait to get to church and announce Anna's arrival. Talk to you later. I want to make some phone calls to the rest of the family."

An added joy was having my mother present for the birth. She had flown out ten days earlier from Ohio. Now Mother, Laz, and I got to spend almost an hour together, just holding the baby and feeling so good about the entire experience. Anna just snuggled close to me. She was very sleepy. I had read that newborns are quite often sleepy and sometimes have a little blue coloring but that this clears up right away and is nothing to worry about. At the time, I didn't notice any blueness and did not suspect that anything was wrong. After seeing that the baby got safely back into the nursery, Mother and Laz went home to rest and to let me get some rest. I tried, but I couldn't.

Around noon they came back. The doctor walked into the room about the same time to inform us that everything was all right, but the baby's coloring was a little blue. He wasn't too concerned at this point; however, he was going to put her in an oxygen tent as a precautionary measure. "Not to worry," he said. "Everything is all right." With that assurance, Mother and Laz went to do some shopping for the baby. They thought I would rest better with them gone for the afternoon. Less than an hour after they had left, the doctor returned to my room with not-so-good news. He said the oxygen wasn't helping Anna and that the oxygen level in her bloodstream still wasn't rising. He felt it was something they needed to check into with X rays and other tests. Would I agree to that?

I was taken totally by surprise. No way to find Mother and Laz, so I said a short prayer and signed the test release papers for the spinal tap. I remember the doctor saying that I looked like I needed a hug and that he was sorry my family was not there. I told him that I would be all right, that I came from strong stock. I guess I was trying to joke so that I wouldn't be so scared. After he left, a nurse came in and held me while I cried a little. She tried to reassure me that this was not serious and that they were doing everything they could to find out exactly why Anna's oxygen level was not rising.

That afternoon was a blur. Of course I couldn't sleep, even though I needed some solid rest. I just wrung my hands and became more and more upset. My roommate, who had had a healthy baby two days before, heard everything that was going on. She came over and held my hand and told me that she was praying for me and Anna. That made me realize that I was not alone. I could lean on and get strength from the Lord. So I prayed that Anna would be all right as I waited for Laz and Mother to return.

Soon the doctor came back. He still didn't know what it was. The chest X ray was vague. He wanted to do another one. They were going to start an IV of fluids and antibiotics just in case it was an infection that was not allowing the oxygen level to rise. He told me that if I didn't remember anything else, to know that I was always allowed to be with the baby and that no questions were dumb questions. He also told me that he wasn't scared yet and that I shouldn't be either. He would let me know when he was, and he promised to be truthful with me at all times.

I can't say enough good things about my pediatrician, Dr. John H. Genrich. Throughout this entire experience, I had complete confidence in him. The nurses at Penrose Hospital were also most caring and thoughtful. Their encouraging words kept me going more than once.

By now it was about four-thirty or five o'clock in the afternoon. I got up. I was a bit dizzy and went into the bathroom. Just then I heard Mother and Laz come in the room joking and laughing. One of them said, "Look, she's flown the coop!"

"No, I'm in here," I called out.

Laz yelled back, "I'm gonna go see our beautiful baby girl. I can't wait."

I knew he didn't know anything that had been going on. I said "No. You wait until I come out." When I entered the bedroom, my Mother took one look at me and said, "Something's wrong." Jan, the nurse who had taken care of me earlier, came in and all of us sat down while I tried to explain everything the doctor was doing for Anna. Jan brought in hospital gowns for each of us, and we walked down to the nursery.

I had not seen Anna for several hours. She looked so little, so different. She now had a tube in her stomach and an oxygen hood that she didn't like and kept fighting. Her legs and arms were pinned down with IVs. The only part of her I could touch was one arm. Now my feelings were quite different from those ecstatic moments in the delivery room. During that wild afternoon I recall at least three different feelings all mixed up, sometimes being expressed, sometimes going unexpressed.

One of them was fear. I was absolutely scared to death. I don't think I have ever been so afraid in my whole life. I was so afraid Anna was going to die, but I couldn't say that out loud. Besides being scared, I tried to deny that this was really happening. I kept thinking that any minute Dr. Genrich would come in the room and tell me that it was all a big mistake. It was another baby that was having problems. Or he would just say that everything was fine and they had gotten worried for nothing. This was something that happened to other people's babies, not mine. Anger was another thing I felt. I was mad that Anna was sick. I was mad that this would happen to her and just plain mad that she was having problems. I was not angry at the doctor or at God, I was just mad in general. The more I thought about it, I was mad at myself. I kept thinking that maybe it was something I had or hadn't done during my pregnancy that could have prevented this. Within twenty-four hours following Anna's birth, my head was crowded with feelings of fear, denial, and anger. It took me several days before I reached acceptance.

At this point another eyewitness picks up Anna's story. It is now approximately twelve hours after the birth. Laurie, Laszlo, and Mary Lou are standing in the hospital hallway outside the nursery talking with Dr. Genrich.

Mary Lou Remembers Anna's Birth

With fear in my heart and tears streaming down my face, I listened to the pediatrician quietly and compassionately explain that even though Anna looked healthy, something was wrong and he was running all kinds of tests to find out what it was. "Oh, no," I cried to myself. "This can't be happening. It's like a nightmare." But somehow, with strength I didn't know I had, I went to my daughter's side and held her in my arms. As I did, my mind was filled with this message: *Trust in the Lord with all your heart and do not rely on your own insight. In all your ways acknowledge him and he will make straight your paths* (Prov. 3:5–6).

All around us was an atmosphere of calm efficiency and of total care for the three of us as well as for Anna. At no time were we made to feel that we were in the way. One nurse even gave me my own box of tissues. Silently the tears came as I talked and prayed and helped make decisions with a clarity that I usually do not have. I knew Anna's chances for living were as great as her chances for dying. I knew that she was getting the best possible medical help, and I knew that the most we could do for Anna was to keep praying. So we did.

As we gathered around Anna in her heated incubator crib, connected to several life-support systems, something prompted me to announce, "Well, gang, we are Christians! We are not alone. Let's pray for Anna." And behind me, Dr. Genrich said, "I think you should. I'm only the helper."

So each of us reached into the crib with our fingertips touching Anna and gave her to God, praying that she would be made whole and well through Jesus Christ.

After praying I went out into the hall still feeling lonely and isolated. My world had suddenly been reduced to one small nursery room with a large window. My husband and the rest of our family still knew nothing of this latest development. I just stood there watching Anna through the window. Suddenly a thought came to me: "Lloyd Nichols is in this hospital!"

Lloyd, a retired United Methodist minister, seminary classmate of my father's, longtime family friend, and the only other person I knew in Colorado Springs was upstairs with his wife Leona who was a patient in the hospital. I phoned her room. He answered and came immediately to the maternity ward. Lloyd stayed with us through the long hours ahead, the first of many Christians to reach out to us in so many ways.

As Lloyd and I stood in the hallway, we saw Laurie go into the nursery and, with the help of the nurse, pick up Anna, tubes, wires, IVs, and all. She began talking to

Anna, but we couldn't hear. All movement stopped in the nursery as heads turned toward mother and daughter.

I went into the room and said, "Laurie, what did you say to the baby?" My beautiful, trusting daughter looked up at me and repeated the words: "Anna, Jesus loves you. Daddy loves you. Mommy loves you. You are God's child and God will take care of you."

I hugged her, tears flowing again, and went out into the hallway to tell Lloyd and Laz. We discussed the possibility of Lloyd baptizing Anna right away, but he suggested we wait until Jim arrived.

Mentally I began making a list of relatives who should be telephoned, but before we could make the calls, Dr. Genrich took us back into Laurie's room and informed us that he was almost certain that Anna had a heart defect of some kind. Although they could do a heart catheterization in Colorado Springs, they were not equipped to do pediatric heart surgery if needed. Therefore, he strongly recommended that Anna be transferred immediately to the University of Colorado Medical Center in Denver, some seventy miles away.

My inner being screamed with pain at the very thought of Anna being separated from her mother, but I knew she must go. As the doctors left the room, Laurie and Laz's good neighbors, Dena and Rudy Bauer, arrived to see the new parents. They, too, listened quietly with tears in their eyes as I explained what was happening. They offered to leave, but I asked them to stay. Knowing of their strong Christian faith, I thought we needed their presence and their support.

The ambulance was called with the special paramedic transport team. Dr. Genrich got permission for Laz to ride in the ambulance with Anna. Before they left, we all gathered for prayer (Laurie, Laz, Dena, Rudy, Lloyd, and I). As we joined hands, hearts, and minds, Lloyd prayed for strength, guidance, and wholeness for all of us and for all the people who would be working with Anna to save her life. We lifted up Laz and Anna who were soon to leave for Denver. We lifted up Laurie who must stay behind for a few days. After this prayer, new hope was born within me and I recalled a familiar hymn:

> O God, our help in ages past,
> Our hope for years to come,
> Our shelter from the stormy blast,
> And our eternal home.

Maxie Dunnam, in his *Workbook of Living Prayer*, talks about "God-incidents"—those unexpected coincidences that just happen, like a burst of insight or an unexplained circumstance that helps us when we need it most—something that happens and can only be indentified as the mysterious workings of God in our lives. For Christians, there are no coincidences, only God-incidents.

I truly believe that Lloyd Nichols's presence in the hospital that night and my happening to see him earlier that day as he got off the elevator were not coincidences, but "God-incidents." The same is true of Rudy and Dena Bauer's arrival at the very moment we needed them.

The body of Christ was beginning to respond to our

need. Prayers were not being prayed in vain. Step-by-step we were being led, guided, and strengthened for what was yet to come. Laz phoned his parents again and shared with them all that was happening. His father, Dr. Laszlo J. Bujdoso, a general surgeon, was extremely helpful and supportive, as was his brother-in-law, Dr. John Wolfe, a pediatrician in San Diego, California. The circle of caring was stretching larger and larger.

As I placed the long-distance call to Ohio to tell my husband Jim, all I got was a busy signal again and again. I called one of our neighbors, Joe Tucker, and asked him to go over to our house and tell my family that something was wrong with the baby. Jim and Toby, our seventeen-year-old son, were sitting down to a late Sunday evening supper when Joe delivered the message. Toby had just returned from a "spring break" week in Florida with church friends. Jim was trying to relax after an exhausting day of church responsibilities, including a wedding.

My words were short and to the point. I asked Jim to fly to Denver immediately to be with Laszlo and the baby. He agreed and said he would call me later to give me his arrival time at the airport. Later Jim told me that when he hung up, Toby, who had heard only one side of the conversation, had asked, "Did Anna die?"

"No, Toby, but they think she has a heart problem and are now moving her to a hospital in Denver. Your mother thinks I should be there. I'm calling TWA right now."

"Is she going to be all right?"

"Too early to tell. Let's sit down, have a word of prayer for Anna, and eat our supper before it gets cold."

"I'm not hungry anymore."

"Neither am I, but we need to pray." And they did.

The transport team from Denver arrived with three paramedics trained and equipped for infant survival. They gently placed Anna in a special incubator loaded with highly sophisticated monitoring devices. As they wheeled the baby into the hall, Laurie reached through one of the access doors and, for a precious short moment, touched Anna. Then she hugged and kissed Laz good-bye, making him promise to call her as soon as he talked with doctors in Denver.

We then moved Laurie into a private room where I could spend the night with her. Sound sleep escaped us, but we did doze off and on through the night. Around 2:00 A.M. the nurse came in. She had a call at the desk from Denver. It was Laz. He had encouraging news. When they arrived they were met by a team of pediatric cardiologists who immediately performed a heart catheterization. The doctors had now diagnosed Anna's problem: Total Anomalous Pulmonary Venous Return.

None of us had ever heard of that before. Laz explained over the phone what the doctors had told him. The blood in her system was going into the wrong side of the heart after returning from the lungs. It should go into the left side, but instead was returning to the right side. All of her pulmonary veins were routed incorrectly. As a temporary measure, the team of doctors had inserted a small balloon through the catheter into the receiving chamber of Anna's heart. By using the inflated balloon, the doctors created a small hole in the wall between the two receiving chambers. This, then, allowed more oxygenated blood to pass through until her heart could be repaired.

The doctors were quite encouraging when they said this could be corrected. It had been done before in small infants. They recommended open-heart surgery as soon as Anna was stable and stronger. The diagnosis explained why Anna was so sleepy and lethargic, why her color was slightly blue, why she had very little energy, and why her oxygen level was abnormal. The doctors assured us that the heart defect was unavoidable, that it had nothing to do with the birthing chair or anything Laurie had or hadn't done during pregnancy.

Later we learned that the University of Colorado Medical Center is one of very few hospitals in the United States equipped to do this rare surgical procedure. It is staffed with doctors who pioneered this medical advance. I call that another "God-incident."

There you have two eyewitness accounts of the facts and feelings surrounding the birth of Anna Bujdoso—Laurie's and Mary Lou's. Her father's story will come later.

However, there is something more I want to share that I found particularly helpful within this first twenty-four-hour period. After that hectic and agonizing Sunday, I finally got to bed around midnight. Here are excerpts from my journal.

Monday, March 29, 1982

12:30 A.M. In bed, but not sleepy. Opened my bed-side Bible and began reading the Book of Psalms and quietly repeating Anna's name for wholeness and healing.

1:00 A.M. Dozed off.

2:00 A.M. Laszlo called informing me that he and Anna had arrived in the Denver Hospital and that the team of pediatric cardiologists was getting ready to do a heart catheterization. He would keep me posted as things developed. I asked him if he was okay. He answered, "Well, we're all upset, but we've put Anna in God's hands. We're praying. I'll call you back."

2:15 A.M. Back to the Bible. I opened to Psalm 91 and God's word spoke directly and reassuringly:

> He who dwells in the shelter
> of the Most High,
> who abides in the shadow
> of the Almighty,
> will say to the Lord,
>
>> "My refuge and my fortress;
>> my God, in whom I trust."
>
> You will not fear the terror of the night.
> No evil shall befall you.
> For he will give his angels charge of
> you.
> Because he cleaves to me in love,
> I will deliver him;

> I will protect him, because he
> knows my name.
> When he calls to me, I will answer him;
> I will be with him in trouble,
> I will rescue and honor him.
> With long life I will satisfy him,
> and show him my salvation.
>
> —Psalm 91, selected verses

As I lay there in the absolute quiet of that moment, I knew I was surrounded by the Holy Spirit and that Anna was also surrounded by God's presence. I read and reread Psalm 91, substituting Anna's name for all the pronouns and visualizing God's angels in charge of her tiny life and her struggling heart.

3:00 A.M.   Dozed off again.

4:00 A.M.   Laszlo called explaining the exact problem and giving me the technical, medical diagnosis. He said the doctors are encouraged. Surgery will be held off for a few days. He suggested I fly out later in the week.

4:15 A.M.   More Bible reading and prayers of thanksgiving.

4:30 A.M.   Went sound to sleep.

6:00 A.M.   Laszlo called again. Anna has stabilized. She is doing much better now that she is getting more oxygen in her system. He has only the highest praise for the attending physicians. Suggested I fly out Wednesday.

6:30 A.M. Got up. Showered, shaved, dressed. Woke Toby and gave him an update on Anna.

7:00 A.M. Sat at the kitchen table sipping my first cup of morning coffee, picked up *The Upper Room* devotional for the day, and read:

> *Monday, March 29, 1982*
> [Jesus] told them a parable, to the effect that they ought always to pray and not lose heart.—Luke 18:1, RSV

> *Thought for the Day*
> God doesn't always come when you want him, but he's always on time.

> *Prayer*
> O Lord, when things seem hopeless and prayer is difficult, help us simply to trust in You and leave the outcome in Your hands. Amen.

Another word of encouragement! Another "God-incident"! Another affirmation of faith! I couldn't wait to call Colorado and tell them what I had just read in *The Upper Room*.

In everything make your requests known to God.

—Philippians 4:6, NEB

2

Prayer:
A Significant Spiritual Therapy

Well-meaning people often come up to me and say, "We've done everything else, now all we can do is pray." It is sad but true that many Christians understand prayer as a last resort rather than our primary resource in combatting illness and in resolving personal problems. Prayers for healing are not human efforts to change God's mind, which has already been revealed to us in Christ. Rather, healing prayer is an effort to change our mind, to draw us closer to God, to make us more receptive and more willing to receive what God has already prepared for us in Christ and through his Holy Spirit. Let me say that another way. When we pray for our own healing or the healing of another, we are not begging God to change his mind; rather, we are intentionally cooperating with God's goodwill for health, wholeness, and salvation.

During those first few hours following Anna's birth, all in our family were offering up prayers of thanksgiving, but when we learned of her heart condition, we added prayers of petition and intercession. We prayed fervently and in faith for Anna's healing. We called The Upper Room Living Prayer Center* in Nashville, Tennessee. The Christian who answered our call not only prayed with us over the phone, but shared our prayer request with three Covenant Prayer Groups in the United States.

Naturally we informed the congregation of the First United Methodist Church in Athens, Ohio. We found within our church family open hearts and an over-whelming outpouring of compassion for little Anna. Just as any crisis within a family tends to draw us all closer together, so it is within the body of Christ. We were being "ministered unto" by God's caring people. We experienced the spiritual truth expressed by the apostle Paul:

> God has so composed the body [the church] . . . that the members may have the same care for one another. If one member suffers, all suffer together; if one member is honored, all rejoice together.
>
> —1 Corinthians 12:24–26

When it became obvious that Anna needed correc-tive heart surgery, the next question was, "How soon?" Her medical team's initial recommendation was to hold

---

*To learn more about the prayer center and how to organize covenant prayer groups, contact The Upper Room, 1908 Grand Avenue, Nashville, Tennessee 37202.

off for several months. Send her home to gain some weight, settle into a daily routine, become a stronger child, then come back to Denver for open-heart surgery. But when Dr. Robert Wolfe realized that Anna lived in Green Mountain Falls, Colorado (altitude 7,800 feet), he quickly changed his thinking. Anna could hardly get through a feeding without going to sleep. Any exertion caused her to tire and become lethargic. The lower oxygen level in Green Mountain Falls increased the risk of sending her home for several months.

The surgery was set for April 13, 1982—just sixteen days after her birth. The risks were high, but we were praying and trusting and hoping for Anna's complete healing.

I felt good about the host of Christians who were concerned and praying for Anna, especially the group that faithfully comes together every Wednesday in the chapel of the First United Methodist Church in Athens. For several years now, the church has offered to the Athens community a worship service of holy communion and intentional healing prayers. God has used the obedience, faith, and availability of that group to help and to heal in many ways. However, Mary Lou, my discerning wife, was not satisfied that we had done everything we could. She strongly suggested that she and I compose a prayer-request letter and mail it immediately to Christian friends and relatives.

"Mary Lou, that sounds like a great idea, but I'm swamped with holy week services and getting everything ready at the church for Easter."

"I know you are busy, but I just feel we must get more Christians intentionally praying for Anna's successful surgery and healing."

"I agree one hundred percent, but don't count on me to help stuff and address envelopes."

"Don't worry, I'll take care of all that. I'll even write the letter, if you and I sign it together."

"How many do you think we should mail out?"

"Seventy-five."

"Okay, let's do it."

Here is the text of the letter mailed on Good Friday, April 9, 1982:

Dear Friends,

We are using this letter to get in touch with you quickly to ask for your prayer support.

Laurie and Laszlo's daughter, Anna Lucille, was born on Sunday, March 28, with a heart condition known as Total Anomalous Pulmonary Venous Return. She was a full-term baby, weighing 7 lbs. 11 oz. She is in the University of Colorado Medical Center at Denver and will have open-heart surgery on Tuesday, April 13.

We are asking you to lift Anna into the light and love of Christ's healing power. She is already a blessing and a miracle to her family. Laurie and Laz need our prayers, too, for strength, patience, and love. They have already witnessed verbally and nonverbally their strong faith in God as their source, to doctors, nurses, and all the people with whom they have come in contact.

Pray for all of us as you have done many times before.

Grace and Peace in Christ,
Mary Lou and Jim Wagner

Almost by return mail, we began to hear from those who received our prayer request letter. Our telephone rang constantly as caring Christians let us know they were praying and that they, in turn, were sharing our letter in their churches, in their prayer groups, and among their friends. Christians of many traditions were indeed lifting up little Anna into the healing light and love of Christ. We heard from Presbyterians, Roman Catholics, Nazarenes, Lutherans, Episcopalians, Pentecostals, Disciples of Christ, and Baptists, as well as Christians in the Assembly of God Church and the Christian and Missionary Alliance Church. The body of Christ extends way beyond one's own local church. We had known that intellectually, but now, thanks to Anna, we experienced it in reality.

Among the dozens of cards, notes, and letters that came to our family were these:

Dear Anna,

I got this note paper from the Easter bunny and it is fun to write with. You are the first one I wrote to. We had to spell dinosaur in spelling. We pray for you a lot because we love you. I know that you aren't having a good Easter, but God will help you and I know it.

From your friend,
Carrie Arnold, age 7
Lima, Ohio

Dear Laszlo and Laurie,

I spoke with your father, Jim, before he left Athens

47

for Colorado. He shared with me about Anna, your daughter. We, at the New Life Assembly of God, have been praying for you and her. Several of our prayer groups, as well as our congregation, are praying. I believe Jesus Christ is the Great Physician. I also believe "all things work together for good to those who love God." Surely you will emerge from this trial with a greater trust in him. My prayer is for Anna's healing and your strength. May God's peace be with you now and forever. May you find his arm strong. His ear attentive. His eye focused on your need. God's grace is sufficient.

Even though we don't know you, we love you. We care.

Love,
John Palmer
Pastor of the Church
Athens, Ohio

From our good friend in Columbus, Ohio, Mrs. Ruth Strickland:

Dear Lord,

Thank you that we may place Anna who is so dear to her mother and father in your loving hands. You love Anna as much as her family does and I affirm that the healing grace of Jesus Christ is now being granted in full measure. And for this I am so very thankful. Thank you, Lord. *Amen.*

These letters of encouragement gave Laszlo and Laurie that extra strength and hope they needed. Perhaps the most unusual, yet the most confirming, message came from Mrs. Elizabeth Wishart, one of Laurie's great-aunts in Tampa, Florida.

We have always been a close family. When we learned that Anna Lucille was born with a dangerous heart condition, we were all praying for her. On Monday, April 12, we received a letter from Mary Lou and Jim (Anna's grandparents), saying she would have open-heart surgery on the 13th. They asked us to "lift Anna into the light and love of Christ's healing power."

On the afternoon of April 14, I was reading the devotional guide in *The Upper Room* and praying for Anna's recovery. The scripture for that day was Ephesians 3:13–21, with special emphasis on the 16th verse in which Paul wrote: "I ask God from the wealth of his glory to give you power through his Spirit to be strong in your inner selves" (TEV).

This encouraged me to pray more.

As I prayed, I remembered an article in the *Reader's Digest* (April, 1980) that I have kept in my night table drawer titled "Six Special Powers of Prayer" by Ardis Whitman. I studied it as I was praying. One of the prayers described in the article is called the "prayer of discovery and contemplation." One thought in it was that so often we think of prayer as a one-way street. We talk to God, but it doesn't seem to occur to us that God talks to us: "How do we pray the prayer of contemplation? In silence, waiting and willing, asking for faith. Not seeing, to see; not hearing, to hear."

I read again *The Upper Room* and prayed more believingly for Anna as God's child. I knew many people were praying for her as I was.

Then came to me a time of quiet peace and beauty, and in my mind I saw many little groups of people praying. There was light and a special feeling above the groups. Words came to my inner being that said, "Anna is going to be all right. My power is sufficient, sufficient, sufficient." The feeling of wonder was there, and I was caught in a sense of gratitude and surety as I realized what had happened. This assurance rested over the many scattered groups of people praying, and a feeling of the words came as an encompassing knowledge of love and power.

This was a new experience for me and thoughts of my unworthiness crept in. Then I read the devotional thought for the next day in *The Upper Room* guide. Across the page I read this prayer: "Friend and Savior, thank You for valuing me so highly. I stand in awe of Your love for me and for others."

That evening I went to the Manhattan Avenue United Methodist Church where I am organist. I did not tell anyone at the two choir rehearsals about this unusual experience as I was still thinking of my unworthiness, wondering, why me?

The next day, I began to realize this was too wonderful to keep to myself. I got in touch with my sisters and then with Mary Lou, Anna's grandmother. When I described over the phone what had happened, she was overjoyed. She explained this as the "confirmation" or answer to our prayers.

We had lifted Anna into the light and love of Christ's healing power and an answer was given. The answer wasn't "she is healed," but rather, "She is going to be all right. My power is sufficient, sufficient, sufficient." Christ's power is sufficient. The connotation of that word had power, love, compassion, understanding, assurance, beauty, and peace. When we pray believingly, and wait in contemplation and silence in God's presence, the blessings will come.

Interesting, is it not, that Elizabeth hesitated before telling anyone about this unusual prayer experience? Was she dreaming, was she awake, was she asleep, was she having an authentic vision? Morton Kelsey is an Episcopal priest who has written extensively on the subject of spiritual phenomena in biblical times and today. In *Dreams: A Way to Listen to God*, he offers the following insights:

> The most significant difference between a dream and a vision is that a dream occurs while we are sleeping and the vision appears while we are awake. A vision is often regarded as an abnormal occurrence, but it really is not. It simply means that a person seeing a vision is open to the same reality entered into in dreams, but in this case he or she is awake. Many people are afraid to admit that they have had visions. . . .
>
> A couple years ago, some psychologists in England tried an experiment. The results showed that out of some 19,000 people, 10 percent admitted to having visions. I remember the day I first gathered all my courage together to give a sermon on dreams and visions. I did not know what the response would be, but after the sermon 25 people came up to me and told me of important dreams and visions they had had which they had never told anyone lest they be labeled mentally ill. They wanted to discuss them, but no one had been ready to listen to them.

I believe Elizabeth experienced a brief but authentic vision the afternoon of April 14, 1982, which indeed proved to be prophetic in the recovery of little Anna.

Could it be that God frequently communicates with us via dreams and visions? Do we receive messages from God in the same way human beings in the Bible did?

Could it be there are some things God either cannot or will not do until people pray? Even to ask this question may be shocking to some. Yet, think of the deeds of mercy, acts of reconciliation, expressions of love, deliberate peace-making behavior in our fractured world. These are works of God accomplished through God's people. In *The Workbook of Intercessory Prayer,* Maxie Dunnam asks, "Why is it such a long leap to think that God is as dependent upon our praying as upon our acting?" He also asks, "What if there are some things God cannot or will not do until people pray?"

Dr. Dunnam points out that "God's promises to act in our lives and in history are often connected with conditions which we must meet. This does not diminish the power and sovereignty of God. Nor does it make God capricious. It simply affirms our relationship with God" and the many opportunities we have to be active participants in the fulfillment of God's kingdom.

Frank Laubach once said, "Prayer is the mightiest power on earth. Enough of us, if we prayed enough, could save the world—if we prayed enough!" According to Dr. Dunnam:

Laubach was far ahead of his time in understanding the power of mind, thought, meditation, and prayer as a source of communicating. He knew that in our praying we do not persuade God to try harder or convince God

of the right answer for a particular problem. Rather . . .
through praying we assist God.

When we pray for others, a mighty spiritual force lifts
our minds and hearts towards God. The Holy Spirit
flows through our prayers to others, enabling God to
speak to them directly. For this reason, Dr. Laubach
sought . . . ten million praying people who would give
themselves to an intentional ministry of prayer. . . .

The need is for a continuous stream of spiritual power
flowing from millions of praying people.

Are you one of those people? God's power will flow
through you to other human beings as you bring them to
God in prayer. You have the privilege every day of
participating in God's redeeming, reconciling, healing
work in our world.

Dr. William S. Jasper, a urologist and practicing physician in Lancaster, Ohio, writing in A New Heart (vol. 7,
no. 1), reveals some intriguing statistics related to 169
patients who had the same surgery (Transvesicocapsular
Prostatectomy). In an article entitled "Aspects of Recovery," he set out to discover what influence, if any, the
patients' spiritual life and faith have in the recovery
process.

There has been a lack of evaluation on the effect of
God's spirit and laws in medicine. Even though some
people pray, have or have not a personal experience
with Jesus Christ, there has been no attempt to determine the effect of these spiritual factors on a patient's
recovery. Patients, families, ministers and church
groups pray for the sick with a faith that God is omnipo-
tent and is the source of recovery and healing for the

sick. God does heal the patient, ease his pain and produce his recovery.

Without God's laws of created regenerated healing in the body, [God's] instruments, such as hospitals, drugs, doctors and other personnel, and the miracles of healing which [God] performs in the incurable and chronically ill, the human race would be hopeless on the planet earth. . . .

If I can prove one operation is better than another one statistically, then I should be able to prove that a Christ related spiritual life is better than a humanistic, temporal life at the time of sickness and surgery. . . .

The patient's response after discharge is the way to determine if the surgical procedure is satisfactory, but what effect did their spiritual life have on these results? [Out of the 169 patients who responded to a survey,] 81% had prayed before surgery, 61% had a personal experience with Jesus Christ and 84% felt their spiritual life helped them in their recovery. The excellent and good results and least complications occurred in those with a strong faith, and complications were tolerated better in those patients with a spiritual relationship. . . .

Those who prayed, those who had a personal experience with Jesus Christ, those who had intercessory prayer had more excellent and good results and less complications. There were twice as many complications in the group who did not have a personal experience with Jesus Christ as those who had.

Recovery and results do not totally depend on the hospital, type of surgery, or the surgeon, but also respond to the spiritual life of the patient, the surgeon, the family, and other personnel involved in the recovery and the cure.

Dr. Jasper's findings correspond with those of another physician reported in the same issue of *A New Heart*. Dr. Graham Clark, noted eye surgeon of New York's Columbia Presbyterian Medical Center, observed what appeared to be a significant difference in the speed of healing, the degree of postoperative pain, and the need for drugs among patients undergoing the same operation. He compiled statistics which revealed that the difference between the fastest and slowest healing in the same surgical procedure is 400 percent.

Interested to discover why there was such a difference among patients, Dr. Clark compared the records of the people in the same age group, equally divided as to sex. Based on his careful study, Dr. Clark concluded "that the committed Christian who is loving, considerate of others, uncomplaining, and has his life centered in Christ, heals far more rapidly, with less pain and less need of drugs, than others."

Prayer, rather than being our last resort, should be our first and primary resource in cooperating with God's therapy in the healing process.

The Lord is near; have no anxiety, but in everything make your requests known to God in prayer and petition with thanksgiving. Then the peace of God, which is beyond our utmost understanding, will keep guard over your hearts and your thoughts, in Christ Jesus.
—Philippians 4:6–7, NEB

A *new heart* I *will give you, and a new spirit* I *will put within you.*

—Ezekiel 36:26

3
Open-Heart Surgery

In Ohio they say, "If you don't like the weather wait until tomorrow because it will probably change." In Denver, Colorado, they say, "If you don't like the weather wait about fifteen minutes because it's sure to change." In April, the "Mile-High City" on the eastern slopes of the Rocky Mountains can be miserably cold with several feet of snow or can have dust storms with summer-like temperatures. "Unpredictable" was the weather report in Denver on April 13, 1982, two days after Easter. "Unpredictable" was the outcome of Anna's open-heart surgery on that spring day.

This chapter is written for everyone who ever felt helpless and inadequate in a hospital waiting room during the surgery of a family member or friend. Anna's waiting party began arriving quite early. First her mother Laurie and her Aunt Kerrie Zeuch around 6:30 A.M. They wanted a few moments alone with Anna before she was taken to the operating room at 7:00 A.M. Shortly thereafter came Anna's father Laszlo and Grandmother Magda Bujdoso. The night before, the four of them had stayed in a nearby motel and were now preparing for the long day in the hospital. Kerrie and Magda found the chaplain's office in that huge complex of buildings called The University of Colorado Medical Center. They left a note with the receptionist to give to the others coming later who would be looking for Anna's waiting room.

Around 9:00 A.M. our good friends from Columbus, Ohio, joined the immediate family. Dave and Joyce Warner had driven out the week before. Dave had already flown back to Ohio for a business trip, but Joyce, her daughter Shari, and her son Scott enlarged the circle of sharing love that day. Scott Warner, a student at the University of Colorado, lives in a Denver suburb and is quite active in the Westminster United Methodist Church. Scott had asked his Christian friends to remember Anna in their prayers. As they were now beginning to settle in and get well acquainted with the decor and furnishings of the waiting room, in walked the Reverend Bruce L. Grauberger, Scott's pastor. The minister sat down and waited with the rest of them.

By midmorning temperatures were in the high sixties. Outside it looked like a good day. Inside the hospital the situation remained unpredictable, as Anna's waiting party thought of ways to pass the time and ways to encourage each other. Kerrie recalls that there were periods of much silence interrupted occasionally with small talk. She remembers, "We did not dwell on the high risks of the surgery, but kept reminding ourselves that we had put Anna in God's hands. We kept trusting that everything would be all right, but the waiting was hard."

Waiting and not knowing the outcome of major surgery is always hard, but we felt that we had done everything humanly possible and that God was truly present and working with the surgical team in repairing Anna's heart.

The Upper Room Living Prayer Center in Nashville had been alerted. Prayer chains and intercessory prayer groups in several churches had been requested to keep Anna in prayer all day. Hundreds of Christians were praying. How many were offering intentional prayer therapy? Only the Lord knows.

Playing cards and table games occupied some of the time for the waiting party. Perhaps the unique happening was Magda's food. When she had landed the day before at Denver's Stapleton International Airport, she deplaned with several suitcases. One was loaded with Hungarian cakes, pastries, bread, sausage, assorted cold meats, and cheese. Magda is an excellent cook. Her theory is that "so long as we are eating, and we keep up our strength, everything will be fine." This theory and practice is applied by Magda in every family crisis. Even though no one had much of an appetite during that morning hospital vigil, Magda's special gifts encouraged everyone and made the time more bearable.

Magda and her husband Dr. Laszlo J. Bujdoso had come to the United States in 1957. Leaving everything behind, they had fled from their beloved Hungary in the wake of the Hungarian revolution and Russian takeover. Dr. Bujdoso, a highly competent surgeon, often recalls the horrid details of escaping across the Hungarian-Austrian border with his wife, his mother, and his two young children. The adults carried twenty-one-month-old Kataline and three-month-old Laszlo G. bundled up on their backs. Through uncharted darkness, climbing barbed wire fences in numbing February temperatures, they ran for their very lives. Gunfire and patrol dogs could be heard nearby. Their only hope for escaping without detection was to make absolutely no noise. Earlier in the evening, Dr. Bujdoso had given each child large quantities of phenobarbital to keep them drugged until they reached safety. However, little Kataline woke up. As she began to cry, her father reached for the pills with one hand, scooped up some snow with the other, and stuffed the contents of both hands into the toddler's mouth. She quickly went back to sleep and did not awaken for many hours.

At another point in their perilous flight an amazing thing happened. The Bujdosos found themselves walking down a hill on ground covered with thin ice. Each footstep broke through the ice, sending loud, crackling sounds into the freezing night air. Magda remembers thinking that the dogs and the guards would surely hear and be upon them any minute. Suddenly, without warning, a strong southern wind began to blow. It howled only a few minutes, just long enough to cover up the noise of their steps breaking the ice, allowing them to pass without being heard by hostile ears.

Arriving in a Vienna refugee camp, they received aid from the Lutheran World Federation. Eventually they booked passage to the United States with the assistance of an organization called International Rescue Service. Temporarily, they lived with relatives in New Brunswick, New Jersey. As soon as possible, all members of the family became American citizens. Dr. Bujdoso completed his required internship and residency program. After passing several state board examinations, he was granted the necessary credentials by the American Medical Association and resumed his medical practice. A third child, Paul, was born in New Jersey in 1965, the same year that the Bujdosos moved to Lisbon, Ohio. They quickly settled into their new American community to raise their three children, providing for them quality educational opportunities that would have been denied in Hungary.

In 1974, Laszlo G. enrolled at Ohio Northern University in Ada, Ohio, to major in business and marketing. Two years later he met and fell in love with Laurie Jo Wagner, a sophomore from Columbus, Ohio, majoring in social work. They were married the summer of 1978, one year before they graduated from O.N.U.

Is it not remarkable that these young people ever met in the first place—Laurie, born in Hondo, Texas, when I was on active duty in the United States Air Force and Laszlo, born in Nyiregyhaza, Hungary, a few months before he and his family escaped the repressive environment of communism? I frequently ask myself, was their chance meeting at Ohio Northern University a coincidence or a "God-incident"?

Now they had a child, a baby with a heart defect. The birth of the first child in any family calls for immediate adjustments in the marriage relationship. The baby demands attention, and the family must set new priorities, even in a healthy-birth situation. Anna's birth and extended stay in the hospital brought added stress and tension to this young marriage. As Laurie commented earlier, "Nothing in my reading or in my prenatal classes prepared me for what to do if the baby is not okay."

Laurie and Laszlo each handled this traumatic event differently. Here is Laszlo's account of his feelings.

Laszlo Remembers Anna's Birth

The day Anna was born and everything seemed to be okay, I remember Mary Lou and I went shopping in the afternoon. When we came back to the hospital we were all bubbly and excited about seeing the baby. We had met the Reverend Lloyd Nichols in the elevator on his way to visit his wife. Mary Lou inquired about her and asked if he had been up to the nursery to see Laurie and Anna. He congratulated us both.

A few minutes later I learned from Laurie and Dr. Genrich that Anna was having some problems, serious problems. I recall leaving the nursery, walking out into the hallway, sitting on the floor, and crying. I was mad. I was drained. I was really down. I just couldn't handle it.

Then I put my hand in my pocket and felt my little aluminum cross. The Reverend Danny Morris had given me that cross a couple years earlier when we were together for a weekend prayer retreat. Inscribed on the cross were the words "Jesus Christ Is Lord." I had gotten in the habit of carrying it in my pocket along with my loose change.

That afternoon in a Penrose Hospital hallway I was upset and angry but, holding my little cross and remembering that Jesus Christ is Lord, I realized that I had no right to be angry, because babies are only loaned to us. Anna belongs to God and I had to trust God to take care of her. Just then Lloyd Nichols appeared in the hallway. We were alone. He just stood there quietly. After a while, I stood up and hugged this wonderful man whom I had just met. With tears in my eyes but a smile on my face, I said to him, "Everything is going to be all right."

Riding to Denver in the ambulance with Anna was hard. Being away from Laurie all that week was hard. Seeing the other babies in that high-risk nursery at the Denver hospital was hard. But there were some happy times, too.

I really enjoyed feeding Anna her bottle. I was the only father in the intensive care nursery. The other babies had mothers and nurses feeding them. Most of the babies in that nursery had been born prematurely. Anna, a full-term baby, looked very big and healthy compared to them. I remember one Mexican-American mother who was there with her baby boy born two months prematurely. He weighed only 1½ lbs. at birth. She would come in every day, reach her hand through the opening in the incubator to touch him, and just cry while she patted his small body.

I sat down next to her and started talking with her. She had pretty much decided that her baby was not going to make it. I found out that there was not a thing wrong with him. He was quite healthy. So I told her about how I had been a "premie" born two months early just like her little boy. I told her I was once about his size, but I had had complications such as lung infection. She turned to me and said, "You don't seem to have anything wrong with you now." I said, "That's right, and neither will he. It just takes a little bit of extra time inside that incubator to get it all together. He'll be just fine."

That seemed to help her and one week later she took her little boy home.

However, I will never forget the one "premie" who didn't make it. The doctors and nurses said the only reason the baby died was because nobody ever came to see him. He didn't get enough love. The nurses tried, but they didn't have the time to spend just with him. After that sad experience, when I wasn't busy with Anna, I went around and talked to all the babies in the nursery who didn't have visitors. I also realized how important it was for me to keep talking to Anna even though she was only a couple of days old. After a while you run out of things to say to a little baby, so I bought a western novel in the gift shop and sat on a little stool by her crib and read to her about the cowboys and Indians and the Old West.

Although I didn't like being separated from Laurie by seventy-five miles, something special happened between Anna and me in those first five days of her life in that intensive care nursery. I lived right there with her, monitoring everything she did and everything they did to her. I remember saying to her more than once, "Oh, Anna, what I would do to change places with you."

Word came to the waiting party around 12:00 noon that the operation was over. The doctor would soon be in to talk with them. Can you imagine the heightened anxiety at that point? Soon Dr. David R. Clarke, Anna's surgeon, came in with an official update.

"We are finished with the surgery. It went very well. We had a small problem when we first tried to take Anna off the heart-lung machine. Had to put her back on for a while, but now her heart is beating on its own. She is going to be just fine. The operation was successful." Then, half-jokingly, Dr. Clark added, "But, of course, she will never become an Olympic runner."

Magda, who had sat quietly all morning, not saying much except when she was passing out food, spoke up boldly to the doctor, "Yes, she will be an Olympic runner. Yes, she will be an Olympic runner."

Lazlo quickly explained to Dr. Clarke that his mother had trained for the Olympic running team when she was a teenager in Hungary, and had actually competed in several international track meets with the top runners in the world. Magda truly believed that someday Anna could be a competitive athlete.

"Oh, I see. Well," continued the doctor, "Anna is now in the recovery room. She will spend the afternoon there before being transferred to the intensive care nursery. Her parents can see her in about an hour. The rest of you will have to wait until later."

With that, Dr. Clarke left the room and Pastor Bruce offered a spoken prayer, thanking God for this good news, for Anna's successful surgery, and for being with them in a special way that day.

All at once everyone was hungry. The minister took off for a luncheon engagement. The three Warners left for a nearby restaurant and the drive back to Boulder, Colorado, where Joyce's parents live. Magda and Kerrie got a bite to eat in the hospital cafeteria, and Laurie and Laszlo went up to the recovery room for their first look at Anna in several hours. Afterwards, Magda and Kerrie took a little walk to relax in the Colorado sunshine. Tensions that had been building for several days began to melt in the warmth of a beautiful spring day.

All reports on Anna were good. Each hour she gained strength. Truly she was in the process of healing. Dr. Clarke's surgical team had rerouted the entire pulmonary vein system to allow the blood to empty into the heart's left atrium. During this complicated procedure, they had also closed the hole previously created in the heart by the balloon when the catheter had been inserted the day she was born. Next came the big question. How long before Anna could check out of the hospital?

The doctors cautiously estimated ten to fifteen days. Because she was doing so well, Kerrie, Joyce, and Shari started back to Ohio. Magda and Laszlo returned to Green Mountain Falls. Laszlo had to go back to work in Colorado Springs, and Magda wanted to get the house ready for the arrival of Laurie and Anna in a couple weeks. Laurie, a bit depressed and lonely after they had gone, kept reminding herself that Anna's worst times were over and that each day was bringing her closer to home and a normal family life.

Words cannot describe Laurie's amazement when Dr. Clarke informed her the next Monday that Anna's progress was so good that he was discharging her immediately. She phoned Laszlo at work, phoned her parents in Ohio, bundled up Anna, put all the suitcases and baby paraphernalia in the car, and drove home singing and laughing and praising God all the way to Green Mountain Falls. Exactly six days after her complicated, intricate, delicate, extensive, open-heart surgery, Anna went home and slept in the cherry cradle her father had made. Her total hospital stay was twenty-two days. She was now on her way to becoming a well baby. Her surgeon, her team of pediatric cardiologists, her pediatrician, and other attending physicians all commented on Anna's accelerated healing and recovery.

My hope is that Anna's story will give encouragement and spiritual motivation to all who read this book and who wonder if their prayers for others really do any good.

Today Anna is a healthy child, growing, developing, and learning that God loved her before she was conscious of God's healing presence. Someday Anna will say with the psalmist:

> For thou, O Lord, art my hope,
>   my trust, O Lord, from my youth.
> Upon thee I have leaned from my birth;
>   thou art he who took me from my mother's womb.
> My praise is continually of thee.
>
> —Psalm 71:5–6

Bless the Lord, O my soul,
    and forget not all his benefits,
who forgives all your iniquity,
    who heals all your diseases.

—Psalm 103:2–3

4
Does God Want to Heal Everyone?

What if Anna's pediatrician had not detected her heart defect? What if the cardiologist had made a miscalculation? What if Anna had not survived the open-heart surgery? What if she had not been healed?

These are some of the hard questions we are now able to discuss. Mary Lou remembers that first day of uncertainty in the hospital: "I knew Anna's chances for dying were as great as her chances for living." Not all critically ill babies are healed, not all survive. Whenever I tell Anna's story, especially in a group setting, invariably someone tells about a baby who did not make it. This chapter is written for those who might ask, "But what about the children, young people, and adults who are not healed? Doesn't God want everyone to be perfectly healthy?"

In this book I am sharing various spiritual therapies that helped our family in cooperating with God's will for Anna's health, therapies that aided our own quest for wholeness. But what about those Christian families who have critically ill loved ones and there is no healing? What happens to a Christian's faith when the expected miracle does not occur?

In Catherine Marshall's autobiography, *Meeting God at Every Turn*, she writes movingly about two of her grandchildren who were seriously ill at birth. Her son Peter telephoned on December 3, 1967. "It's a boy, Mom." But his voice was not as excited as a man's should be over his first child. "Something's wrong, Mom. 'Poor muscle tone,' the doctors say." Severe lung congestion followed, then the threat of pneumonia.

Loving hands of Christian friends were laid on the baby, praying for a miracle. A few days later the infant died and his grandmother, struggling with her own emotions, wrote: "Lord, I don't understand. When Peter Marshall died, Your sure word to me was that 'goodness and mercy' would follow me all the days of my life. Lord, is this goodness and mercy?"

Two and a half years later, a perfectly healthy baby girl was born to Peter and Edith Marshall. This time the grandmother wrote in her journal, "Thank you, Lord. Forgive me for my doubts."

Then, on July 22, 1971, a third child was born to Peter and Edith. It was apparent from day one that little Amy Catherine had suffered severe damage to her internal organs. The doctors called it "genetic aberration cerebrohepatorenal syndrome." They offered no hope, medically, but the Marshall family felt called to pray in faith, asking God for a miraculous healing. Wrote the grand-mother this time:

> If ever a family went out on the end of a limb of faith, we did. As for me, not since Peter Marshall's first heart attack had I thrown everything I am and have, every resource of spirit and mind and will, into the battle for a human life.

Ten close Christian friends flew in to be with the family and join them in prayer; churches around the country were alerted and asked to pray for little Amy and her family. Six weeks after her birth, the baby died. For the next six months, Catherine Marshall experienced the most intense misery she had ever known and found herself asking: "What can we really believe about healing through prayer? How can God permit such things to happen? If he is a loving God, surely he would not want such evils to befall us."

In *Tracks of a Fellow Struggler*, John R. Claypool, minister of the Broadway Baptist Church in Fort Worth, Texas, has written of his personal anguish and loss in the death of his daughter.

> For almost two decades, I had served as a pastor and often participated in the drama of suffering and death, but it was always happening to someone else. I could sympathize, but never really empathize. However, no one can live on this earth very long without being initiated into the fraternity of the bereaved.

Pastor Claypool relates that his first acquaintance with grief was when he sat by the bedside of his father-in-law as he went through his final stages of life. Then, shortly afterwards, the wife of one of his closest friends died.

> Yet it was not until part of my own flesh and blood—my eight-year-old daughter, Laura Lue—was diagnosed with acute leukemia that "my time came," and I was thrust inside the trauma of living with and through the misery of dying.

The Claypools naturally and intentionally turned to God in faith, expecting God's healing love to rid the child of her fatal illness. When the disease went into periods of remission, John Claypool remembers:

> I pondered whether or not she had been totally healed by God. I had prayed for this many times, and hundreds of other people had done the same thing. I certainly believe such is possible.

Laura Lue lived only eighteen months and ten days after her diagnosis. Out of his intense grief and sorrow, her father wrote:

> There is more honest faith in an act of questioning than in the act of silent submission, for implicit in the very asking is the faith that some light can be given. . . .
> I do not believe God wants me to hold in these questions that burn in my heart and soul—questions like: "Why is there leukemia? Why are children of

promise cut down at the age of ten? Why did You [God] let Laura Lue suffer so excruciatingly and then let her die?"

The mystery of why some are healed and some are not continues to go unanswered. Rabbi Harold S. Kushner's book, *When Bad Things Happen to Good People*, gets the reader's attention with this opening statement:

> There is only one question which really matters: why do bad things happen to good people? All other theological conversation is intellectually diverting; somewhat like doing the crossword puzzle in the Sunday paper and feeling very satisfied when you have made the words fit; but ultimately without the capacity to reach people where they really care. Virtually every meaningful conversation I have ever had with people on the subject of God and religion has either started with this question, or gotten around to it before long.

As a Christian pastor, I, too, have engaged in many intellectual exercises with people who want to know but never discover satisfying answers to their "why" questions.

Then there are those well-meaning friends who try to comfort us with unhelpful answers.

"Be brave. God has a plan and purpose in all this."

"You are being punished for some sin."

"Maybe God is trying to teach you a lesson."

"This is God's will. Just accept it."

"Even though you can't see it now, someday you will understand God's reason for all this."

"Hang on. God is testing your faith."

"Be strong. God won't send you more than you can handle."

In her book, *The Bereaved Parent,* Harriet Sarnoff Schiff recalls:

> When her young son died during an operation to correct a congenital heart malfunction, her clergyman took her aside and said, "I know that this is a painful time for you. But I know that you will get through it all right, because God never sends us more of a burden than we can handle. God only let this happen to you because He knows that you are strong enough to bear it."

Her reaction to these words: "If only I was a weaker person, Robbie would still be alive."

Perhaps in those moments of intense grief, it is far better to remain silent and simply "be with" our heavy-hearted friends, empathetically sharing their pain. Notice that many people responding to tragedy have at least one thing in common—they assume that the cause of our suffering is God. According to Rabbi Kushner:

> There may be another approach. Maybe God does not cause our suffering. Maybe it happens for some reason other than the will of God. The psalmist writes, "I lift mine eyes to the hills; from where does my help come? My help comes from the Lord, maker of Heaven and earth" (Psalm 121:1–2). He does not say, "My pain comes from the Lord," or "my tragedy comes from the Lord." He says, "my *help* comes from the Lord."

I like best the rabbi's concluding chapter entitled, "What Good, Then, Is Religion?" Here he affirms that God does not cause our misfortunes and that the question we should be asking is not, "Why did this happen to me?" or "What did I do to deserve this?" These are unanswerable and pointless questions. The more productive question would be, "Now that this has happened to me, what am I going to do about it?"

In Romans 8:28 we see that this is clearly the theological direction in which Paul leads the church: "We know that in everything God works for good with those who love him, who are called according to his purpose." Notice the Apostle does not say, "We know that God causes everything to happen to us." God allows us to make our own choices. God permits our human wills to operate freely. Therefore, much of life is in response to the consequences of that freedom. Likewise, much of life is in response to circumstances and events beyond our personal control, such as accidents, disease, natural disaster, violence, and crime. Rather than blame God, the Bible teaches us to respond to God in times of tragedy and trauma with trust and confidence.

O God, because I know you care about me and you want only the best for me, I want to cooperate with you in all circumstances. Help me to keep on keeping on; to not give up, and to be faithful to you, to my family, to my friends, and to my church. I take my stand with Paul and say to you, O God, even in this dark moment in my life, that I know you will eventually bring forth some good because you alone are good, you are completely reliable, you are worthy of my trust and confidence.

This is the same spiritual truth that arose in Mary Lou's consciousness the day Anna was born: "Trust in the Lord with all your heart, and do not rely on your own insight. In all your ways acknowledge him, and he will make straight your paths" (Prov. 3:5–6). The title for this chapter, "Does God Want to Heal Everyone?" raises a significant question. Throughout Christian history God has demonstrated a desire to help and to heal all people. Why, then, do many Christians back away from this happy truth?

Dennis Bennett, an Episcopal priest and pastor of St. Luke's Church in Seattle, Washington, writes in *Sharing* (May, 1983):

> If I allow the idea that there are some people that God does not want to heal, then not many are healed, because each person has the thought in his or her mind, "Perhaps I am the one God doesn't want to heal, perhaps God has some purpose in keeping me sick," and so he or she is hindered from really taking hold of God's promise. I don't believe we are going to see more than a trickle of healing until we have really settled it in our minds that God indeed wants to heal us—that there is no doubt about it.

As a Christian, I truly believe that God does want to heal everyone. I want to cooperate in every way with

God's goodwill and gracious love not only for my own wholeness, but also for the total health of all God's children. My strong hunch is that most people reading this chapter title assume what I am really asking is this: "Does God want physical healing for everyone?" Even to that question I say, "Yes, God's intentional will is for all of us to enjoy excellent physical health." However, I also ask that the reader understand "healing" in a holistic way. What good is a perfect body if spiritual health is lacking? What good is a miraculous physical healing if we can't get along with other people? The healing that God desires for each of us includes but goes beyond physical health. God also desires for each of us the healing of broken relationships; emotional problems; negative attitudes; wounded memories; debilitating worry, fear, and anxiety; and the healing of grief and guilt.

Furthermore, we cannot separate our various illnesses into neatly labeled categories. Human nature is so complex that sickness in one part of our personality affects all the other parts. Medical and psychological researchers are discovering that an extremely high percentage of physical illnesses have a nonphysical origin.

Emily Gardner Neal gives perspective to our total health needs in *The Lord Is Our Healer*:

> No one who properly understands spiritual healing ever turns from God because he is not healed, for no one who turns to Him in faith remains unhealed spiritually. Further, no one who has experienced a healing of the

spirit would exchange what he has received for a purely physical cure.

The basic healing and the greatest healing is spiritual. When one knows deep within the peace of God that passes all understanding, one is able to cope creatively with all kinds of illnesses. In the traditional language of Christianity, this spiritual healing goes by several names: salvation; getting right with God; reunion with the Creator; regeneration via the second birth; born again; or being saved through Jesus Christ.

Robert T. Standhardt is a quadriplegic minister and a dynamic witness to God's will for wholeness. Because of a birth injury, he must use a walker or a wheelchair wherever he goes. Writing in *The Upper Room Disciplines 1982*, he notes that

the greatest disabling conditions that persons face are often not the external physical problems, but the ones inside, in the mind and the heart. As a person with an obvious physical handicap, I have seen people cross to the other side of the street rather than meet me, sit in front of and behind me, and talk all around me in church, and otherwise treat me as if I were unfeeling.

Then there are other times (not often enough) when someone will look me in the eye (although they may have to kneel to do this), talk *with* me rather than *to* me, sit beside me, and not be afraid to take my hand and communicate that the person accepts and affirms me simply as a person. This is the touch that makes me whole inside, that breathes the Spirit into me. When we touch each other in such love and respect, wholeness comes as Christ's touch becomes our own.

Even though Robert Standhardt is physically disabled, he is an effective Christian minister and quite healthy, mentally and spiritually. God's normative will is that everyone be healed; however, often there are countervailing factors that hinder total health. When such is the case, we do not submit to hopeless resignation; rather, we continue to pray for God's help, continue to support and cooperate with God's goodwill, continue to employ all of God's health care delivery systems.

Having a healthy relationship with God or having a wholeness of the spirit is the essence of abundant life. Yet, because physical health is so highly prized by human beings, many people not only seek it at all costs, but tend to see it as the very essence of life. A Christian should understand physical health in a broader perspective and not as the epitome of existence.

Consider these three statements:

1. All human beings are terminal, physically speaking.

   Our Creator did not design or program the body to last forever. Physical death is an inescapable reality for each person.

2. All physical healing is temporary.

   Even a miraculous, dramatic healing does not

guarantee permanent health. It is only a matter of time before another malfunction or breakdown of one or more of a person's physical systems.

3. All Christians are a resurrection people.

   Physical death is not the end of life, but a transition to more life, to ultimate healing, to perfect wholeness, and to complete harmony with God. For this reason, we pray for each other's total healing, even in the face of physical death, lifting each other up into the light and love of the Divine Physician, cooperating with God's will for wholeness on both sides of death.

Yes, we even proceed in this faith-act when the doctor pronounces that awesome phrase, "terminal illness." Do not think of "terminal" as a hopeless, dead-end track; rather imagine "terminal" as a place where you exchange one form of transportation for another in order to continue your journey.

Leona Nichols, beloved wife of the Reverend Lloyd Nichols, our good friend in Colorado, died after a lengthy struggle with cancer in August, 1982. In his pain of separation and grief, Lloyd said to us, "She crossed over peacefully. She was ready. I thank God for each day we had together. And I thank God for the many, many Christians who ministered to us in so many ways." Leona Nichols exchanged one form of transportation for another in order to continue her journey.

Jane Scott, a good friend in Athens, Ohio, died at age fifty-eight after losing a long battle with cancer. There was standing room only in the Presbyterian church sanctuary the afternoon of her funeral, as the community gathered to honor Jane and to thank God for this vibrant Christian lady. Let me share with you a letter I wrote to her husband Charles a few days after her death.

Dear Charles,

I want to tell you how much Jane ministered to me each time I visited her and had prayer with her. Specifically I want to share with you a little bit about my last visit with her on March 18, 1983.

I arrived at the hospital around 11 A.M. She was alone, awake, and seemed to be at ease and resting. I didn't stay long—maybe fifteen minutes. We talked about many things. As I looked around her room and saw all the photographs on the walls, children's hand-made greetings from her school, and many fresh flowers, I commented, "All around you I see evidence of much love." To this she responded, "That's because God is love."

Jane also said to me, "Every day is beautiful. I thank God for each day, even though I cannot move my body. I can move my arms and hands. I praise the Lord and thank him every day."

Even though Jane, for reasons beyond our comprehension, was not healed physically, she was totally healed in her spirit, her mind, her relationships with

God and people. I believe the healing Christ has now given her perfect wholeness in every way.

We are keeping you in our prayers during these days of adjustment.

Grace and Peace in Christ,
Jim Wagner

Jane was not "terminal"; rather, Jane had reached a point in her existence where she exchanged one form of transportation for another in order to continue her eternal journey. I believe this also holds true for Laura Lue Claypool and for Catherine Marshall's grandchildren.

God does want to heal everyone. God actively offers us wholeness, health, and salvation on both sides of death. This is why our Lord Jesus Christ gave us his assurance:

I am the resurrection and the life; he who believes in me, though he die, yet shall he live, and whoever lives and believes in me shall never die. Do you believe this?
—John 11:25–26

For the promise is to you and to your children and to all that are far off, every one whom the Lord our God calls to him.

—Acts 2:39

5

Baptism: Anna's and Ours

The Mountain View United Methodist Church (a most appropriate name) lies on the outskirts of Woodland Park, Colorado, elevation 8,465 feet. To the east rises the Rampart Range, to the west the Collegiate Range, and almost due south the granddaddy of the Rocky Mountains, Pike's Peak, topping out at 14,110 feet. Pastor Phillip Green, Jr., says that every time he views these three majestic creations of God, it reminds him of the Holy Trinity. My first visit was on August 11, 1982, the day of Anna's baptism. Driving into that magnificent setting, I found myself silently repeating Psalm 121:1–2.

> I lift up my eyes to the hills.
> From whence does my help come?
> My help comes from the Lord,
> who made heaven and earth.

Organized in 1978, this mission church met for three-and-a-half years in the music room of the Woodland Park Junior High School. During that formative period, several United Methodist ministers from the Colorado Springs area provided pastoral care and conducted worship services. The most regular of these pioneering ministers is our friend Dr. Lloyd C. Nichols, a retired District Superintendent, regarded by many in the congregation as their "patron saint."

Phil Green is now the full-time minister of this young and growing Christian community that moved into a fully-equipped new church building early in 1982. Laszlo and Laurie had been looking for a church home and, at the gracious invitation of Lloyd Nichols, they had visited the Mountain View church, only eight miles from their home in Green Mountain Falls. They found the pastor and the people genuinely open and receptive to area residents and visitors. Soon they arranged to have their church membership transferred from the Sharon Park United Methodist Church in Lima, Ohio.

Whether or not to baptize Anna was never an issue. The only question was when to baptize. Again, God's timing is best. I was so thankful for the decision not to baptize her that first hectic day in the hospital. The sacrament of holy baptism is a corporate act of the church, a joyous occasion in the worship life of the congregation, a special moment of initiation and entry into the household of faith, and a unique opportunity for family reunion and family sharing.

It had taken some juggling of vacation schedules and

other commitments, but somehow both sets of parents, Laszlo's brother Paul, and Laurie's brother Toby were able to gather with the Mountain View congregation for this time of celebration. To say I was thrilled with the thought of baptizing my own granddaughter is quite an understatement.

The gathering worshipers in that midsummer service were in a festive, happy mood. The weather had been perfect all week. The mountains surrounding the church radiated grandeur, strength, and stability. The aspen paneling in the sanctuary complemented the gorgeous natural setting. All the preparations were complete. All the participants were ready. The candles had been lit, the organ music had begun, the baptismal bowl had been filled with water from the Jordan River. The three ministers (Pastor Green, Dr. Nichols, and myself) entered from the narthex and took seats in the chancel.

Pastor Green warmly welcomed all of us, led the call to worship, and read the scripture lessons while baby Anna slept peacefully on her father's lap. I couldn't help but praise God with an overflowing heart as I looked at this four-and-a-half-month-old child, fully recovered from her open-heart surgery. Anna had already brought love and joy into her family. I wondered what God had in store for her future.

My thoughts temporarily left the Mountain View church as I remembered another midsummer service on August 26, 1978, at the First United Methodist Church in Athens, Ohio. Mentally I did a quick replay of escorting Laurie Wagner down that long center aisle to be married to Laszlo Bujdoso. That, too, had been a festive time of celebrating God's love and goodness. Now their marriage had been blessed with the birth of Anna.

Suddenly I was overwhelmed with the reality of God's grace at work in their lives and in the lives of all Christians, and I remembered some lines from "Amazing Grace":

> Through many dangers, toils, and snares,
> I have already come;
> 'Tis grace hath brought me safe thus far,
> And grace will lead me home.

God's amazing grace (unmerited, undeserved love) was truly present in that baptismal service.

Although some Christians question the validity and appropriateness of baptizing infants, this has never been an issue in our family. All three of our children had been baptized within a few weeks after we brought them home from the hospital. In the Methodist tradition we are quite orthodox in believing that baptism is the port of entry into the Christian family of God; however, parents have the option of having their babies baptized or delaying that decision until the children are older and can share in that sacred commitment. Immersion, pouring, and sprinkling are the traditional methods used in our church. Whether the candidate for baptism is sixty years old or six days old, the meaning and significance of this sacramental action is the same. Whether the officiating minister uses a river-full or a cup-full of water, the symbolism is the same.

When parents call my office requesting infant baptism, I place in their hands a well-written pamphlet by William H. Willimon titled "Your Child Is Baptized." I want to share with you one of the author's excellent illustrations.

When we were born, we were given our family name. On the day of our birth we had no idea what that name meant, what all it included, what relatives, responsibilities, traditions, gifts, and tasks it might entail. Nevertheless, we were as much a member and participant in our family as we would ever be. It was given to us at our birth into our family. What remained was for us to grow day by day into an increasing, broadening awareness of what that name meant for us and our life. We have learned what it means as we have shared meals with our family, been instructed in family traditions and values, and observed older members of the family as they went about living their lives. In a thousand big and small ways we grow into our families, increasingly affirming and becoming for ourselves what had been given to us at birth.

In the same way, when we are baptized, at whatever age, we are given the name *Christian*. We are recognized as full members of the family of God and made heirs to God's gracious gifts in Jesus Christ. The child cannot know all that the name *Christian* implies or demands. Nevertheless, on this baptismal day, your child is given everything he or she will ever need to be God's beloved child. What remains is for the child to grow, day by day, through countless conversations, repentings, discoveries, and rebirths into an increasing awareness of what this name really means for living the life of faith.

Always we are dependent upon God to do for us what we cannot do for ourselves. Water, sacraments, mothers, fathers, family members, Christian friends, the church, and prayer are employed by the Holy Spirit to bring about fulfillment to the baptized ones. From the day of baptism on, whenever a child asks, "Who am I?" Christian parents can respond as Laurie said to Anna, "You are God's child and God will take care of you."

Dr. Nichols was introduced and stepped into the pulpit to present the baptismal message. Even though I had known this Christian gentleman all of my married life, only since Anna's birth had we become close friends. Lloyd was a seminary classmate and good friend of Mary Lou's father, the Reverend Lorin Stine, back in the late 1920s and early 1930s. When my father-in-law was killed in a tragic accident in 1958, it was Lloyd who had come to preach the funeral service and comfort us in our terrible grief.

Now, twenty-four years later, this tall, strong, compassionate man of Christ continued to minister to our family. Officially, he is supposed to be retired. Unofficially, he will never retire. When he prays, when he preaches, when he counsels, the spirit of Christ is evident in his personality. Even though he has passed his eightieth birthday, each Sunday finds him "filling in" as a guest minister. Lloyd's message on the occasion of

Anna's baptism reveals his pastoral heart, and I want to share with you part of that message:

> I can think of nothing more helpful than the two scriptures just read, Psalm 91 and Mark 10:13–16. I had the privilege of being with this family the day in which faith needed to be there also, the day Anna was born.
>
> Psalm 91 is a psalm of faith and a psalm of trust. On that day I found faith in these two young people and in Mary Lou. I believe it was because of this faith, along with the help of all the doctors, that Anna is with us tonight in good health. In talking to Mary Lou that evening after the ambulance had come from Denver to take Anna and Laszlo to another hospital, I was amazed at the calmness of this family. You see, God works in so many different ways, through so many different people. Mary Lou talked to me and I said to her, "I feel all right, I feel it is all right." I know they also had some deep assurances.
>
> Psalm 91 is a profound psalm of faith. The author found the only security he had was in the shadow of the almighty God. He looked every other place for security, but he could not find it. So it is with each one of us. We can turn to each other and find help and strength, but the real help comes from God, who comes to us in our hearts through our Lord Jesus Christ, giving us security beyond human reason. . . .
>
> In the scripture lesson from Mark's Gospel, Jesus is rebuking the disciples for not bringing the little children to him. "Let the children come to me, do not hinder them; for to such belongs the kingdom of God" (Mark 10:14). The greatest prayer that Jesus ever taught us says, "Thy kingdom come, Thy will be done, on earth

as it is in heaven" (Matt. 6:10). This is Jesus' dream, yet he says the kingdom will come into the world as we become like little children. . . . Think how a little child is so dependent upon parents and others. We, too, must become this dependent on Jesus. He also says we must be as receptive of this gift that he gives us, as the child is receptive of the love that parents give. . . .

Yes, amazing things happen through faith. How do we receive some of these miracles? I think it is through prayer. Prayer is the most powerful force in all the world. Jesus depended upon prayer for his own power. Jesus received his power from talking with God. The apostles knew this. They saw and heard Jesus in prayer. They didn't ask him to teach them to preach. They didn't ask him to show them how to perform miracles, but they did say, "Lord, teach us to pray" (Luke 11:1).

Do you know the power of prayer in your own life? I saw it in the lives of Anna's family. I saw the power of prayer in their lives, even with all of the turmoil. And it stirred my heart! . . .

Laurie and Laszlo come here tonight to have Anna baptized and to show their gratitude and commitment to God. . . . I pray that each one of us and that these parents will be known by our prayer life in the bringing up of Anna. It is my privilege to be here with you in these moments and to express a word of thanks to God for giving us this little loved one along with these precious friends. May God bless you. *Amen.*

Following Lloyd's beautiful message, Pastor Green asked Laurie and Laszlo to come forward with Anna, along with all the family members present. The parents responded to the "sacred promises" and then the pastor addressed this special word to Anna.

"Little Child, for you Jesus Christ came into the world. For you he has triumphed over death. But you, Little Child, do not yet know anything about this. In the meantime, believe the Bible that teaches us, 'We love God because God first loved us.'"

As Laszlo handed me the baby, she began to fuss a bit. I invited all the family members and the other two ministers to lay hands on Anna as I asked the question, "What name is given this child?"

Her parents responded, "Anna Lucille."

The water from the Jordan River trickled down her head as I pronounced the historic blessing.

"Anna Lucille, I baptize you in the name of the Father, and of the Son, and of the Holy Spirit. *Amen.*"

Afterword

As I searched through the rows of Valentine cards looking for the right one, my only objective was to find a greeting with a cat on it. Next to balloons and "draws" (her word for crayons), Anna's favorite subject is cats. The sales clerk tried to help me in my quest. Soon we were involved in a grandmother-to-grandmother conversation. I found my card, oversized with a kitten sitting in a bucket, the caption reading: *Valentine, I'm stuck on you!*

As I paid for my card, the friendly woman said, "Where does your granddaughter live?"

"In Colorado," I replied.

"Oh," she said, "how sad!"

I left the store feeling more than a little sorry for myself. How we would love to see her more often! My thoughts went back to those first three difficult weeks and then instead of focusing on "How sad!" I concentrated on "Where does your granddaughter live?" Praise God, Anna lives! Not where we can see her very often, but live she does—laughing, playing, and learning things the hard way just like any other almost-two-year-old.

As I think about all the ways Anna's life has affected our lives, I am overwhelmed with God's goodness and with the love God poured out to all of us through the body of Christ. When we were the most discouraged, someone always appeared or called or wrote or sent something.

The day I took Laurie home from the hospital was wild. After a six-day bout with a kidney infection, she was released from Penrose Hospital in Colorado Springs (the baby was in a Denver hospital).

As we got into the car, an unusually powerful wind was roaring down the mountain passes into the city. Then we noticed that some hospital windows and car windows had been shattered by the impact. The radio reported gusts up to one hundred miles per hour. Knowing that Jim, Laz, Joyce, and Dave were on their way from Denver driving in a van in that extremely high wind was little consolation. The night before I had tried to get the house ready for Laurie's homecoming. As I worked, I found myself moving baby clothes and infant things thinking, "O dear Lord, if Anna doesn't live what am I going to do with all this?"

Just then the phone had rung. It was my stepsister Mary Ellen Case from Vandalia, Ohio, with this message: "Now, I know you're tired and discouraged and it's not over yet, but quit thinking about the 'what if's and concentrate on what you're doing now. I think Anna is going to make it."

Now I remembered Mary Ellen's words and concentrated on driving up the pass in the terrible wind. Somehow we made it to Green Mountain Falls. As we pulled up to the house we were joyfully and tearfully greeted by our husbands and the Warners. Much to our delight, Dave Warner had gone into the Denver hospital nursery and taken a videotape of Anna. Not having seen her since she was sixteen hours old, Laurie and I sat with tears running freely, realizing in full that she was still alive. New hope for Laurie and for all of us.

Because Anna's condition at birth was so precarious, I had put away the little pink clothes I had bought and had not even shown them to Laurie. A stuffed animal from the Bauers was all she had received in the way of gifts. It was as if we were all holding our collective breaths. But now as we watched the videotape, Jim brought out a package beautifully wrapped with pink paper and ribbon.

"Here, Laurie. A package from the Hendersons and Florence."

These dear friends in our church in Athens are so thoughtful, yet, I wondered if this was the appropriate moment to open it. Now I did hold my breath and anxiously watched my daughter as she unwrapped the gift with excitement much as she had when she was a little girl. In the folds of tissue paper lay an exquisite pink dress with matching slippers.

Without hesitation Laurie exclaimed, "Oh, look! Anna has an Easter dress."

Miriam Henderson, who usually gives practical gifts like receiving blankets and diapers, had been nudged, I believe, by the Holy Spirit to give Anna something to wear in public soon. The size was 0–3 months. I watched my daughter relax and smile for the first time in nearly a week, and I breathed a prayer of thanksgiving.

These were some of the immediate pictures that flashed into my mind after I purchased Anna's Valentine card. Then it seemed as though God opened a floodgate of beautiful thoughts as I continued to recall other ways Anna's experience had touched our lives.

In James 5:16, we read, "Pray for one another, that you may be healed." At the first reading it would seem that the "you" only refers to the sick person. Could it also refer to the person doing the praying? I think it does. Through our experience of praying for Anna, our own lives were touched and healed in many different ways.

Six months after Anna's surgery, my mother and I stood in a crowd of cheering people watching runners cross the finish line of the Athens, Ohio, "Indian Summer Six-Mile Run." The October sun was hot. The temperatures and the humidity that afternoon were unseasonably high. Several runners had passed out as they finished. We were waiting for Jim and Toby, who were running together. That Toby, age seventeen, was competing was no surprise, but the fact that Jim, age forty-eight, was running in a race for the first time in his life was truly amazing.

I became increasingly concerned as runners straggled in. Prayer arose within me, "Lord, help them finish the race. Six months ago Jim couldn't run six minutes, now here he is trying to go six miles. Lord, help Toby and Jim to encourage each other along the way."

Suddenly someone from the crowd yelled, "Look, here come Toby and Jim Wagner!"

And look I did as Toby grabbed his dad's hand and lifted it in a sign of victory as they crossed the finish line together!

During one of Jim's private prayer times six months earlier, he had been praying for Anna when this question came to him: "Will I be alive when Anna graduates from high school?" Odd question since Anna was only a few days old and fighting for her life in the Intensive Care Unit. But the question persisted and caused him to focus on his own health—body, mind, and spirit. As he did an inventory of himself, he came to grips with what many of his family members and friends had been concerned about for a long time. Jim had developed a paunch! True, he was not obese, but overweight, yes. He was out of breath occasionally and lacked the energy to do the things he had to do each day.

Anna's birth into our family became the catalyst for Jim's enrollment in the adult physical fitness program at Ohio University. Now, here he was six months later, crossing the finish line of a six-mile run, giving the glory to God, weighing thirty-five pounds lighter, and enjoying a great moment of comradery with our son.

Another person who was blessed and encouraged

through praying for Anna was Jim's grandmother, Anna Blanche Wheatley Stone. Grandma Stone wrote this letter to Anna on December 3, 1982:

My Dear Little Baby Anna,

I am writing you this little letter although I know you cannot read or understand it now, but perhaps your Mommy and Daddy will keep it for you until you are old enough to understand about me. I am so happy they named you Anna for that is a very good name. I have carried it for 93 years and now it is your turn to keep the name alive. It was my grandmother's name.

I pray for you daily that you will grow up to be a sweet and lovely lady. I don't expect to ever see you, but I can think about you and pray for you and your Mommy and Daddy. I am praying that you will grow up loving the Lord and that you will obey your parents. I am writing these things because I know I will never be able to say them to you. So, Darling Baby, I will say good-bye to you now. There are many other things I would love to tell you but it is so hard for me to write. I will just keep on praying for you until God calls me home. Be a good and happy girl. I love you although I have never seen you.

Your Great-Great-Grandmother Stone

In June, 1983, Jim, Laurie, Anna, and I flew to Fort Myers, Florida, to visit Jim's mother, Lillian Wagner, and her mother, Anna Blanche Stone. It was a beautiful visit. Great-Grandma Stone did not tire of watching Anna play around her chair and having Anna sit on her lap. She announced that now she wanted to be called Grandma Anna! The trip was a gift from Jim's mother, but the best gift was seeing Grandma Anna with Baby Anna. Life is a fragile and precious gift. How thankful we are that we could spend this brief time in Florida with our family.

As various family members gathered the materials for this book, we had an opportunity to reflect on the impact of it all. Laszlo's question to Laurie helped us maintain perspective and focus: "What do you want this book to do?" Laurie's answer speaks for all in the family.

"I want this book to be a proclamation of how God works, and about God's healing power. I want it to give hope to other people who may be in a similar situation." This book is a "passing on" to others of the strength, encouragement, and comfort we received. Paul speaks of God as the One

> who comforts us in all our affliction, so that we may be able to comfort those who are in any affliction, with the comfort with which we ourselves are comforted by God.
> —2 Corinthians 1:4

Our family benefited greatly from God's comfort given to us by other caring persons. Our hope is that the Comforter will use this book to help others cope, endure, and overcome. Anna's trauma and triumph has been a learning-growing experience for all in her family. We have renewed appreciation for these truths:

Life is too fragile and too precious to be taken casually and for granted.

Prayer is not the last resort, but the first line of defense and the most effective offense God has instilled within the human heart.

People come first, material things are a lesser priority.

Family love is a special kind of love, not to be taken lightly or neglected, but rather to be nurtured intentionally.

The local church community is an extended family for each Christian; therefore, the church-family needs to be more sensitive to all persons in crises, especially to those who have little or no natural family.

We are comforted by God, not only for our sakes, but also to be a comfort (a source of strength) to others.

One of the strengths of the Christian healing ministry is that God has many delivery systems to channel health, wholeness, and salvation.

Today is Saturday—"Omelette Day"—the only day in the week we have a leisurely, late breakfast. Kerrie and David have already called to say they are coming to Athens for the day. Before this day is over we will, no doubt, talk to Toby at Otterbein College (in Westerville, Ohio, where he is a freshman), and to Laurie and Laz in Colorado. What joy we experience through our family. The phone rings and before I can say "hello," a little voice says, "Hi, Nana, I wuv you."

"Hi, Anna, I love you."

Yes, Anna, Jesus loves you. We all love you. Truly you are God's child. God has cared for you in the past, is caring for you now, and will care for you tomorrow.

Yea! (Anna's word for *Amen.*)

Mary Lou Wagner

From the Family Album

Jim Wagner, Allison Bujdoso, Laurie Bujdoso, Laszlo Bujdoso, Anna Bujdoso, and Mary Lou Wagner.

About the Author

Jim Wagner is Director of The Upper Room Prayer and Healing Ministries and also Executive Director of the Disciplined Order of Christ. He received his Doctor of Ministry degree from United Theological Seminary in Dayton, Ohio.

Before assuming his present position with The Upper Room, Dr. Wagner was Senior Minister of First United Methodist Church in Athens, Ohio. He has long had a special interest in the healing ministry of the church. His experiences as a pastor engaged in intentional healing ministries with several congregations are shared in *Blessed to Be a Blessing,* a study guide to help local churches organize and maintain healing services based on holy communion.

Dr. Wagner and his wife Mary Lou have three children. They now have two grandchildren, Anna and her sister Allison.